THE TRUMPET OF CONSCIENCE

THE TRUMPET OF CONSCIENCE

by

MARTIN LUTHER KING

HODDER AND STOUGHTON

Copyright © 1967 by Martin Luther King, Jr.
Introduction copyright © 1968 by Coretta Scott King

First printed in Great Britain 1968
Third impression 1970

ISBN 0 340 10957 2

Printed in Great Britain for Hodder and Stoughton Limited,
St. Paul's House, Warwick Lane, London, E.C.4 by
Hazell Watson & Viney Ltd, Aylesbury, Bucks

FOREWORD

When the Canadian Broadcasting Corporation invited my husband to give the 1967 series of Massey Lectures over their radio network, the assignment was for him to talk about anything he considered of importance, of relevance not only to the United States but to the world at large.

The subjects to which Martin Luther King, Jr., decided to address himself were those uppermost in his mind during the past years and months: his conclusion that nonviolent protest had to evolve into actions of civil disobedience; his conviction that our role in the Vietnam war demanded closer scrutiny and stronger resistance; his thoughts about the role which our awakened youth—both black and white—might play in the shaping of a new world. The final lecture of the series was scheduled for Christmas Eve—and committed preacher that he was, Martin Luther King, Jr., preached "A Christmas Sermon on Peace"—addressing his congregation in Atlanta, Georgia, from the pulpit of Ebenezer Church, but knowing that his dream for world peace was shared by all men of goodwill, the world over.

Martin Luther King, Jr.—black leader—was a man for all people. The killers of the dream could end his mortal existence with a single bullet, but not all the bullets in all the arsenals can effect his death. We will not have to search for him. Listen for him in the protests of the poor—black and white. Look for him in the places where social evils are nonviolently resisted by proud, brave people. Listen for him in the ever-increasing chorus of committed individuals. Remember him as a man who tried to be "a drum major for justice, a drum major for peace, a drum major for righteousness." Remember him as a man who refused to lose faith in the ultimate redemption of mankind.

Coretta Scott King

May 1, 1968

CONTENTS

The five talks published in this book were broadcast during November and December, 1967, over the Canadian Broadcasting Corporation as the seventh annual series of Massey Lectures. The lectures are named in honour of the late Rt. Hon. Vincent Massey, former Governor General of Canada.

I

IMPASSE
IN
RACE
RELATIONS

TODAY, when progress has abruptly stalled and hope withers under bitter backlashing, Negroes can remember days that were incomparably worse. By ones and twos more than a century ago Negroes groped to freedom, and its attainment, by a pitiful few, sustained hundreds of thousands as the word spread through the plantations that someone had been reborn far to the north.

Our freedom was not won a century ago, it is not won today; but some small part of it is in our hands, and we are marching no longer by ones and twos but in legions of thousands, convinced now it cannot be denied by any human force.

Today the question is not whether we shall be free, but by what course we will win. In the recent past our struggle has had two phases. The first phase began in the early fifties when Negroes slammed the door shut on submission and subservience. Adapting nonviolent resistance to conditions in the United States, we swept into Southern streets to demand our citizenship and manhood. For the South, with its complex system of brutal segregation, we were inaugurating a rebellion. Merely to march in public streets was to rock the *status quo* to its roots. Boycotting buses in Montgomery, demonstrating in Birmingham, the citadel of segregation, and defying guns, dogs, and clubs in Selma, while maintaining disciplined nonviolence, totally confused the rulers of the South. If they let us march, they admitted their lie that the black man was content. If they shot us down, they told the world they were inhuman brutes. They tried to stop us by threats and fear, the tactics that had long worked so effectively. But nonviolence had muzzled their guns and Negro defiance had shaken their confidence. When they finally reached for clubs, dogs, and guns, they found the world was watching, and then the power of nonviolent protest became manifest. It dramatized the essential meaning of the conflict and, in magnified strokes, made clear who was the evildoer and who was the undeserving victim. The nation and the world were sickened and through national legislation wiped out a thousand Southern laws, ripping gaping holes in the edifice of segregation.

Those were days of luminous victories. Negroes and whites collaborated for human dignity. But there was a limitation to our achievements.

Negroes were outraged by inequality; their ultimate goal was freedom. Most of the white majority were outraged by brutality; their goal was improvement, not freedom nor equality.

When Negroes could use public facilities, register and vote in some areas of the South, find token educational advancement, again in token form find new areas of employment, it brought to the Negro a sense of achievement, but it brought to the whites a sense of completion. When Negroes assertively moved on to ascend the second rung of the ladder, a firm resistance from the white community developed. This resistance characterized the second phase, which we are now experiencing. In some quarters it was a courteous rejection, in others it was a stinging white backlash. In all quarters unmistakably it was outright resistance.

The arresting of the limited forward progress by white resistance revealed the latent racism that was deeply rooted in U.S. society. The short era of widespread goodwill evaporated rapidly. As elation and expectations died, Negroes became more sharply aware that the goal of freedom was still distant, and our immediate plight was substantially still an agony of deprivation. In the past decade little had been done for Northern ghettos. All the legislation was designed to remedy Southern conditions—and even these were only partially improved. A sense of futility and frustration spread and choked against the hardened white attitudes.

Nonviolence as a protest form came under attack as a tactical theory, and Northern Negroes expressed their dismay and hostility in a succession of riots.

The decade of 1955 to 1965 with its constructive elements misled us. Everyone underestimated the amount of violence and rage Negroes were suppressing and the amount of bigotry the white majority was disguising.

The riots are now in the centre of the stage, and are being offered as basis for contradictory positions by whites and Negroes. Some Negroes argue they are the incipient forms of rebellion and guerrilla tactics that will be the feature of the Negro revolt. They are represented as the new stage of Negro struggle replacing the old and allegedly outworn tactic of nonviolent resistance. At the same time, some white forces are using riots as evidence that Negroes have no capacity for constructive change and in their lawless behaviour forfeit all rights and justify any form of repressive measures. A corollary of this theory is the position that the outbursts are unforgivable, ungrateful, and menace the social order.

I would like to examine both questions: Is the guilt for riots exclusively that of Negroes, and are they a natural development to a new stage of struggle?

A million words will be written and spoken to dissect the ghetto outbreaks, but for a perceptive and vivid expression of culpability I would sub-mit two sentences written a century ago by Victor Hugo:

> If the soul is left in darkness, sins will be committed. The guilty one is not he who com-mits the sin, but he who causes the dark-ness.

The policy-makers of the white society have caused the darkness; they created discrimination; they created slums; they perpetuate unemploy-ment, ignorance, and poverty. It is incontestable and deplorable that Negroes have committed crimes, but they are derivative crimes. They are born of the greater crimes of the white society. When we ask Negroes to abide by the law, let us also declare that the white man does not abide by law in the ghettos. Day in and day out he violates welfare laws to deprive the poor of their meagre allotments; he flagrantly violates building codes and regulations; his police make a mockery of law; he violates laws on equal employment and education and the provisions for civic services. The slums are the handiwork of a vicious system of the white society; Negroes live in them, but they do not make them, any more than a prisoner makes a prison.

Let us say it boldly that if the total slum viola-tions of law by the white man over the years were calculated, and were compared with the law-breaking of a few days of riots, the hardened criminal would be the white man.

In using the term "white man" I am seeking to describe in general terms the Negro's adversary. It is not meant to encompass all white people. There are millions who have morally risen above prevailing prejudices. They are willing to share power and to accept structural alterations of society even at the cost of traditional privilege. To deny their existence as some ultra-nationalists do is to deny an evident truth. More than that, it drives away allies who can strengthen our struggle. Their support not only serves to enhance our power, but in breaking from the attitudes of the larger society it splits and weakens our opposition. To develop a sense of black consciousness and peoplehood does not require that we scorn the white race as a whole. It is not the race *per se* that we fight but the policies and ideology that leaders of that race have formulated to perpetuate oppression.

To sum up the general causes of riots, we would have to say that the white power structure is still seeking to keep the walls of segregation and inequality substantially intact, while Negro determination to break through them has intensified. The white society, unprepared and unwilling to accept radical structural change, is resisting firmly, and thus producing chaos because the force for change is vital and aggressive. The irony is that the white society ruefully complains that if there were no chaos great changes would come, yet it creates the circumstances breeding the chaos.

Within the general cause of riots it is possible to identify five specific elements: (1) *the white backlash;* (2) *pervasive discriminatory practices;* (3) *unemployment;* (4) *war in Vietnam;* and (5) *urban problems and extensive migration.*

The white backlash is a primary cause because it explains the ferocity of the emotional content of the outbursts and their spontaneity. Negroes have endured insults and humiliation for decades and centuries, but in the past ten years a growing sensitivity in the white community was a gratifying indication of progress. The depravity of the white backlash shattered the hope that new attitudes were in the making. The reversion to savage white conduct marked by a succession of murders in the South, the recrudescence of white hoodlumism in Northern streets, and coldly systematic withdrawal of support by some erstwhile white allies constituted a grim statement to Negroes. They were told there were firm limits to their progress, that they must expect to remain permanently unequal and permanently poor; they were warned not to confuse cautiously measured improvements with expectation of full equality.

The white backlash declared true equality could never be a reality in the United States.

The pervasiveness of discriminatory practices is so taken for granted that its provocative effect is readily forgotten. There are generational differences in character among Negroes. The older generation has substantially inured itself to daily insults, but a younger generation has a lower threshold of tolerance. The thousands of fences, visible and invisible, that confine Negroes to restricted neighbourhoods, schools, jobs, and social activity incite an intensely hostile reaction in the young. They have rejected the old way and cannot be soothed and tranquillized by promises of a new way in some distant future. Discrimination cuts off too large a part of their life, to be endured in silence and apathy.

Even when a Negro manages to grasp a foothold on the economic ladder, discrimination remains to push him off after he has ascended a few rungs. It hounds him at every level, to stultify his initiative and insult his being. For the pitiful few who climb into economic security it persists and closes different doors to them.

Intimately related to discrimination is one of its worst consequences—unemployment. The United States teetered on the edge of revolution in the 1930s when unemployment ranged up to 25 per cent. Today in the midst of historic prosperity unemployment for Negro youth, according to government figures, runs as high as 30 to 40 per cent in many cities. With most of their lives yet to live, the slamming of doors in their faces can be expected to induce rage and rebellion.

The fourth cause is the war in Vietnam. Negroes are conscripted in double measure for combat. They constitute more than 20 per cent of the front-line troops in a war of unprecedented savagery although their proportion in the population is 10 per cent. They are marching under slogans of democracy, to defend a Saigon government that scorns democracy. At home they know there is no genuine democracy for their people, and on their return they will be restored to a grim life as second-class citizens even if they are bedecked with heroes' medals.

Finally, a complex of causes are found in the degenerating conditions of urban life. The cities are gasping in polluted air and enduring contaminated water; public facilities are outworn and inadequate; financial disaster is an annual crisis. Within this chaos of neglect, Negroes are stifled at the very bottom, in slums so squalid their equal is not to be found in any other industrial nation of the world.

Most of the largest cities are victims of the large migration of Negroes. Although it was well known that millions of Negroes would be forced off the land in the South by the contraction of agricultural employment during the past two decades, no national planning was done to provide remedies. When white immigrants arrived in the United States in the late nineteenth century, a beneficent government gave them free land and credit to build a useful, independent life.

In contrast, when the Negro migrated, he was left to his own resources. He crowded the cities and was herded into ghettos, left in unemployment, or subjected to gross exploitation within a context of searing discrimination. Though other minorities had encountered obstacles, none was so brutally scorned or so consistently denied opportunity and hope as was the Negro.

All of these conditions were the fuel for violence and riots. As the social psychologist, Kenneth Clark, has said, it is a surprise only that outbreaks were not experienced earlier. There are many thoughtful social scientists who are now acknowledging that the elements of social catastrophe have accumulated in such vast array that no remedies may be available.

I am not sanguine, but I am not ready to accept defeat. I believe there are several programmes that can reverse the tide of social disintegration, and beyond that I believe that destructive as the riots may be they have been analysed substantially in a one-sided fashion.

There is a striking aspect to the violence of the riots that has stimulated little comment and even less analysis. In all the riots, taken together, the property damage reached colossal proportions (exceeding a billion dollars). Yet the physical injury inflicted by Negroes upon white people was inconsequential by comparison. The bruising edge of the weapon of violence in Negro hands was employed almost exclusively against property —not persons.

It is noteworthy that many distinguished periodicals and leaders of the white community, even while the conflict raged, in clear terms accepted the responsibility for neglect, evasion, and centuries of injustice. They did not quibble nor did they seek to fasten exclusive culpability on the Negro. They asked for action and a facing-up to the need for drastic social reformation. It is true that not all were motivated by morality. The crisis of Negro aspirations intersects with the urban crisis. Some white leaders may not be moved by humanity to save Negroes, but they are moved by self-interest to save their cities. But even their moral and selfish motives, which merge toward a constructive end, have not yet made the government act. It is preoccupied with war and is determined to husband every resource for military adventures rather than for social reconstruction.

Negroes must therefore not only formulate a programme, but they must fashion new tactics which do not count on government goodwill but serve, instead, to compel unwilling authorities to yield to the mandates of justice.

We are demanding an emergency programme to provide employment for everyone in need of a job or, if a work programme is impracticable, a guaranteed annual income at levels that sustain life in decent circumstances. It is now incontestable that the wealth and resources of the United States make the elimination of poverty perfectly practicable.

A second feature of our programme is the demolition of slums and rebuilding by the population that lives in them.

There is scarcely any division among Negroes for these measures. Divisions arise only around methods for their achievement.

I am still convinced that a solution of nonviolence remains possible. However, nonviolence must be adapted to urban conditions and urban moods. The effectiveness of street marches in cities is limited because the normal turbulence of city life absorbs them as mere transitory drama quite common in the ordinary movement of masses. In the South, a march was a social earth-quake; in the North, it is a faint, brief exclamation of protest.

Nonviolent protest must now mature to a new level to correspond to heightened black impatience and stiffened white resistance. This higher level is mass civil disobedience. There must be more than a statement to the larger society; there must be a force that interrupts its functioning at some key point. That interruption must not, however, be clandestine or surreptitious. It is not necessary to invest it with guerrilla romanticism. It must be open and, above all, conducted by large masses without violence. If the jails are filled to thwart it, its meaning will become even clearer.

The Negro will be saying, "I am not avoiding penalties for breaking the law—I am willing to endure all your punishment because your society will not be able to endure the stigma of violently and publicly oppressing its minority to preserve injustice."

Mass civil disobedience as a new stage of struggle can transmute the deep rage of the ghetto into a constructive and creative force. To dislocate the functioning of a city without destroying it can be more effective than a riot because it can be longer-lasting, costly to the larger society, but not wantonly destructive. Finally, it is a device of social action that is more difficult for the government to quell by superior force.

The limitation of riots, moral questions aside, is that they cannot win and their participants know it. Hence, rioting is not revolutionary but reactionary because it invites defeat. It involves an emotional catharsis, but it must be followed by a sense of futility.

Where does the future point? The character of the next period is being determined by the response of white decision-makers to this crisis. It is a harsh indictment, but it is an inescapable conclusion, that Congress is horrified not at the conditions of Negro life but at the product of these conditions—the Negro himself. It could, by a single massive act of concern expressed in a multibillion-dollar programme to modernize and humanize Negro communities, do more to obviate violence than could be done by all the armies at its command. Whether it will summon the wisdom to do it is the question of the hour.

It is a shattering historical irony that the American Revolution of 1776 was the consequence of many of the same conditions that prevail today. King George adamantly refused to share power even in modest degree with the colonies. He provoked violence by scorning and spurning the appeals embodied in nonviolent protests such as boycotts, peaceful demonstra-

tions, and petitions. In their resort to violence
the colonists were pressed ideologically beyond
their original demands and put into question the
system of absolute monarchical rule. When they
took up arms and searched for the rationale for
independence, they broke with all traditions of
imperial domination and established a unique
and unprecedented form of government—the
democratic republic.

The Negro revolt is evolving into more than a
quest for desegregation and equality. It is a challenge, to a system that has created miracles of
production and technology, to create justice. If
humanism is locked outside of the system,
Negroes will have revealed its inner core of
despotism and a far greater struggle for liberation
will unfold. The United States is substantially
challenged to demonstrate that it can abolish,
not only the evils of racism, but also the scourge
of poverty of whites as well as of Negroes and the
horrors of war that transcend national borders
and involve all mankind.

The first man to die in the American Revolution was a Negro seaman, Crispus Attucks. Before
that fateful struggle ended, the institution of
absolute monarchy was laid on its death bed.

We may now be in only the initial period of an
era of change as far-reaching in its consequences
as the American Revolution. The developed in-

dustrial nations of the world cannot remain secure islands of prosperity in a seething sea of poverty. The storm is rising against the privileged minority of the earth, from which there is no shelter in isolation and armament. The storm will not abate until a just distribution of the fruits of the earth enables man everywhere to live in dignity and human decency. The American Negro of 1967, like Crispus Attucks, may be the vanguard in a prolonged struggle that may change the shape of the world, as millions of deprived shake and transform the earth in their quest for life, freedom, and justice.

II

CONSCIENCE
AND THE
VIETNAM
WAR

IT is many months now since I found myself obliged by conscience to end my silence and to take a public stand against my country's war in Vietnam. The considerations which led me to that painful decision have not disappeared; indeed, they have been magnified by the course of events since then. The war itself is intensified; the impact on my country is even more destructive.

I cannot speak about the great themes of violence and nonviolence, of social change and of hope for the future, without reflecting on the tremendous violence of Vietnam.

Since the spring of 1967, when I first made public my opposition to my government's policy, many persons have questioned me about the wisdom of my decision. "Why *you*?" they have said. "Peace and civil rights don't mix. Aren't you hurting the cause of your people?" And when I hear such questions, I have been greatly saddened, for they mean that the inquirers have never really known me, my commitment, or my calling. Indeed, that question suggests that they do not know the world in which they live.

In explaining my position, I have tried to make it clear that I remain perplexed—as I think everyone must be perplexed—by the complexities and ambiguities of Vietnam. I would not wish to underrate the need for a collective solution to this tragic war. I would wish neither to present North Vietnam or the National Liberation Front as paragons of virtue, nor to overlook the role they can play and the successful resolution of the problem. While they both may have justifiable reasons to be suspicious of the good faith of the United States, life and history give eloquent testimony to the fact that conflicts are never resolved without trustful give-and-take on both sides.

Since I am a preacher by calling, I suppose it is not surprising that I had several reasons for bringing Vietnam into the field of my moral vision. There is at the outset a very obvious and almost facile connection between the war in Vietnam and the struggle I and others have been waging in America. A few years ago there was a shining moment in that struggle. It seemed as if there was a real promise of hope for the poor, both black and white, through the Poverty Programme. There were experiments, hopes, new beginnings. Then came the build-up in Vietnam, and I watched the programme broken and eviscerated as if it were some idle political plaything of a society gone mad on war, and I knew that America would never invest the necessary funds or energies in rehabilitation of its poor so long as adventures like Vietnam continued to draw men and skills and money like some demoniacal destructive suction tube. And so I was increasingly compelled to see the war not only as a moral outrage but also as an enemy of the poor, and to attack it as such.

Perhaps a more tragic recognition of reality took place when it became clear to me that the war was doing far more than devastating the hopes of the poor at home. It was sending their sons and their brothers and their husbands to fight and to die and in extraordinarily higher proportions relative to the rest of the population. We were taking the black young men who had been crippled by our society and sending them eight thousand miles away to guarantee liberties in Southeast Asia which they had not found in southwest Georgia and East Harlem. And so we have been repeatedly faced with the cruel irony of watching Negro and white boys on TV screens as they kill and die together for a nation that has been unable to seat them together in the same schools. We watch them in brutal solidarity burning the huts of a poor village, but we realize that they would never live on the same block in Detroit. I could not be silent in the face of such cruel manipulation of the poor.

My third reason moves to an even deeper level of awareness, but it grows out of my experience in the ghettos of the North over the last three years —especially the last three summers. As I have walked among the desperate, rejected, angry young men, I have told them that Molotov cocktails and rifles would not solve their problems. I have tried to offer them my deepest compassion, while maintaining my conviction that social change comes most meaningfully through non-violent action. But, they asked, and rightly so, what about Vietnam? They asked if our own nation wasn't using massive doses of violence to solve its problems, to bring about the changes it wanted. Their questions hit home, and I knew that I could never again raise my voice against the violence of the oppressed in the ghettos without having first spoken clearly to the greatest purveyor of violence in the world today: my own government. For the sake of those boys, for the sake of this government, for the sake of the hundreds of thousands trembling under our violence, I cannot be silent.

For those who ask the question, "Aren't you a civil rights leader?"—and thereby mean to exclude me from the movement for peace—I answer by saying that I have worked too long and hard now against segregated public accommodations to end up segregating my moral concern.

Justice is indivisible. It must also be said that it would be rather absurd to work passionately and unrelentingly for integrated schools and not be concerned about the survival of a world in which to be integrated. I must say further that something in the very nature of our organizational structure in the Southern Christian Leadership Conference led me to this decision. In 1957, when a group of us formed that organization, we chose as our motto: "To save the soul of America." Now it should be incandescently clear that no one who has any concern for the integrity and life of America today can ignore the present war.

As if the weight of such a commitment were not enough, another burden of responsibility was placed upon me in 1964: I cannot forget that the Nobel Prize for Peace was also a commission—a commission to work harder than I had ever worked before for "the brotherhood of man". This is a calling which takes me beyond national allegiances, but even if it were not present, I would yet have to live with the meaning of my commitment to the ministry of Jesus Christ. To me the relationship of this ministry to the making of peace is so obvious that I sometimes marvel at those who ask me why I am speaking against the war. We are called to speak for the weak, for the voiceless, for the victims of our nation, and for those it calls enemy, for no document from human hands can make these humans any less our brothers.

And as I ponder the madness of Vietnam and search within myself for ways to understand and respond in compassion, my mind goes constantly to the people of that peninsula. I speak now not of the soldiers of each side, not of the junta in Saigon, but simply of the people who have been living under the curse of war for almost three continuous decades now. I think of them, too, because it is clear to me that there will be no meaningful solution until some attempt is made to know them and to hear their broken cries.

They must see the Americans as strange liberators. The Vietnamese people proclaimed their own independence in 1945 after a combined French and Japanese occupation and before the Communist revolution in China. They were led by Ho Chi Minh. Even though they quoted the American Declaration of Independence in their own document of freedom, we refused to recognize them. Our government felt then that the Vietnamese people weren't ready for independence, and we again fell victim to the deadly Western arrogance that has poisoned the international atmosphere for so long.

For nine years, following 1945, we vigorously supported the French in their abortive effort to

recolonize Vietnam. After the French were defeated, it looked as if independence and land
reform would come through the Geneva Agreements. But instead there came the United States,
determined that Ho should not unify the tem-
porarily divided nation, and the peasants watched
again as we supported one of the most vicious
modern dictators, our chosen man, Premier Diem.
The peasants watched and cringed as Diem ruth-
lessly rooted out all opposition, supported their
extortionist landlords, and refused even to discuss
reunification with the North. The peasants
watched as all this was presided over by U.S. influence and then by increasing numbers of U.S.
troops, who came to help quell the insurgency
that Diem's methods had aroused. When Diem
was overthrown, they may have been happy, but
the long line of military dictatorships seemed to
offer no real change, especially in terms of their
need for land and peace.

The only change came from America, as we in-
creased our troop commitments in support of
governments which were singularly corrupt, in-
ept, and without popular support. All the while,
the people read our leaflets and received regular
promises of peace and democracy—and land reform. Now they languish under our bombs and
consider us—not their fellow Vietnamese—the
real enemy. They move sadly and apathetically as

we herd them off the land of their fathers into concentration camps where minimal social needs are rarely met. They know that they must move or be destroyed by our bombs, and they go, primarily women and children and the aged. They watch as we poison their water, as we kill a million acres of their crops, and they wander into the hospitals with at least twenty casualties from American fire power to one Vietcong-inflicted injury. They wander into the towns and see thousands of children homeless, without clothes, running in packs on the streets like animals. They see the children selling their sisters to our soldiers, soliciting for their mothers.

What do the peasants think, as we ally ourselves with the landlords, and as we refuse to put any action into our many words concerning land reform? Where are the roots of the independent Vietnam we claim to be building? Is it among these voiceless ones?

We have destroyed their two most cherished institutions: the family and the village. We have destroyed their land and their crops. We have co-operated in crushing one of the nation's only non-Communist revolutionary political forces, the United Buddhist Church. We have supported the enemies of the peasants of Saigon. We have corrupted their women and children and killed their men. What liberators!

Now there is little left to build on—save bitterness. And soon the only solid physical foundations remaining will be found at our military bases and in the concrete of the concentration camps we call fortified hamlets. The peasants may well wonder if we plan to build our new Vietnam on such grounds as these; could we blame them for such thoughts? We must speak for them, and raise the questions they cannot raise. These, too, are our brothers.

Perhaps the more difficult but no less necessary task is to speak for those who have been designated as our enemies. What of the National Liberation Front? How can they believe in our integrity when now we speak of "aggression from the North" as if there were nothing more essential to the war? How can they trust us when now we charge them with violence after the murderous reign of Diem? And charge them with violence when we pour every new weapon of death into their land? Surely we must understand their feelings, even if we do not condone their actions. How do they judge us when our officials know that their membership is less than 25 per cent Communist, and yet insist on giving them the blanket name? They ask how we can speak of free elections when the Saigon press is censored and controlled by the military junta. Their questions are frighteningly relevant. Is our nation planning to build on political myth again and then shore it up with the power of new violence?

Here is the true meaning and value of compassion and nonviolence, when they help us to see the enemy's point of view, to hear his questions, to know his assessment of ourselves. For from his view we may indeed see the basic weaknesses of our own condition, and if we are mature, we may learn and grow and profit from the wisdom of the brothers who are called the opposition.

So, too, with Hanoi. In the North, where our bombs now pummel the land and our mines endanger the waterways, we are met by a deep but understandable mistrust. In Hanoi are the men who led the nation to independence against the Japanese and the French. It was they who led a second struggle against French domination, and then were persuaded to give up the land they controlled between the 13th and 17th parallels as a temporary measure at Geneva. After 1954 they watched us conspire with Diem to prevent elections which would surely have brought Ho Chi Minh to power over a united Vietnam, and they realized they had been betrayed again.

When we ask why they do not leap to negotiate, these things must be remembered. Also, it must be clear that the leaders of Hanoi consider the presence of American troops in support of the Diem regime to have been the initial military breach of the Geneva Agreements concerning foreign troops. They remind us that they did not begin to send in any large number of supplies or men until American forces had moved in to the tens of thousands. Hanoi remembers how our leaders refused to tell us the truth about the earlier North Vietnamese overtures for peace, how we claimed that none existed when they had clearly been made. Ho Chi Minh has watched as America has spoken of peace and built up its forces, and now he has surely heard the increasing international rumours of American plans for an invasion of the North.

At this point, I should make it clear that while I have tried in these last few minutes to give a voice to the voiceless on Vietnam and to understand the arguments of those who are called enemy, I am as deeply concerned about our own troops there as anything else. For it occurs to me that what we are submitting them to in Vietnam is not simply the brutalizing process that goes on in any war, where armies face each other and seek to destroy. We are adding cynicism to the process of death, for they must know after a short period there that none of the things we claim to be fighting for are really involved, and the more sophisticated surely realize that we are on the side of the wealthy and the secure while we create a hell for the poor.

If we continue, there will be no doubt in my mind and in the mind of the world that we have no honourable intentions in Vietnam. It will become clear that our minimal expectation is to occupy it as an American colony, and men will not refrain from thinking that our maximum hope is to goad China into a war so that we may bomb her nuclear installations.

Somehow this madness must cease. We must stop now. I speak as a child of God and brother to the suffering poor of Vietnam. I speak for those whose land is being laid waste, whose homes are being destroyed, whose culture is being subverted. I speak for the poor of America who are paying the double price of smashed hopes at home and death and corruption in Vietnam. I speak as a citizen of the world, for the world as it stands aghast at the path we have taken. I speak as an American to the leaders of my own nation. The great initiative in this war is ours. The initiative to stop it must be ours.

In the spring of 1967, I made public the steps I consider necessary for this to happen. I should add now only that while many Americans have supported the proposals, the government has so far not recognized one of them. These are the times for real choices and not false ones. We are at the moment when our lives must be placed on the line if our nation is to survive its own folly.

Every man of humane convictions must decide on the protest that best suits his convictions, but we must all protest.

There is something seductively tempting about stopping there and going off on what in some circles has become a popular crusade against the war in Vietnam. I say we must enter that struggle, but I wish to go on now to say something even more disturbing. The war in Vietnam is but a symptom of a far deeper malady within the American spirit.

In 1957 a sensitive American official overseas said that it seemed to him that our nation was on the wrong side of a world revolution. I am convinced that if we are to get on the right side of the world revolution we as a nation must undergo a radical revolution of values. A true revolution of values will soon cause us to question the fairness and justice of many of our past and present policies. A true revolution of values will soon look uneasily on the glaring contrast between poverty and wealth. With righteous indignation, it will look across the seas and see individual capitalists of the West investing huge sums of money in Asia, Africa, and South America only to take the profits out with no concern for the social betterment of the countries, and say: "This is not just." It will look at our alliance with the landed gentry of Latin America and say: "This is not just." The

Western arrogance of feeling that it has everything to teach others and nothing to learn from them is not just. A true revolution of values will lay hands on the world order and say of war: "This way of settling differences is not just." This business of burning human beings with napalm, of filling our nation's homes with orphans and widows, of injecting poisonous drugs of hate into the veins of peoples normally humane, of sending men home from dark and bloody battlefields physically handicapped and psychologically deranged, cannot be reconciled with wisdom, justice, and love. A nation that continues year after year to spend more money on military defence than on programmes of social uplift is approaching spiritual doom.

This kind of positive revolution of values is our best defence against Communism. War is not the answer. Communism will never be defeated by the use of atomic bombs or nuclear weapons.

These are revolutionary times; all over the globe men are revolting against old systems of exploitation and oppression. The shirtless and barefoot people of the land are rising up as never before. "The people that walked in darkness have seen a great light." We in the West must support these revolutions. It is a sad fact that because of comfort, complacency, a morbid fear of Communism, and our proneness to adjust to injustice, the

Western nations that initiated so much of the revolutionary spirit of the modern world have now become the arch-antirevolutionaries. This has driven many to feel that only Marxism has the revolutionary spirit. Therefore, Communism is a judgment against our failure to make democracy real and follow through on the revolutions that we initiated. We must move past indecision to action. We must find new ways to speak for peace in Vietnam and for justice throughout the developing world, a world that borders on our doors. If we do not act, we shall surely be dragged down the long, dark, and shameful corridors of time reserved for those who possess power without compassion, might without morality, and strength without sight.

III

YOUTH
AND
SOCIAL
ACTION

WHEN Paul Goodman published *Growing Up Absurd*, in 1960, he electrified the public with his description of the shattering impact on the young generation of the spiritual emptiness of contemporary society. Now, years later, it is not spiritual emptiness that is terrifying, but spiritual evil.

Today, young men of America are fighting, dying, and killing in Asian jungles in a war whose purposes are so ambiguous the whole nation seethes with dissent. They are told they are sacrificing for democracy, but the Saigon regime, their ally, is a mockery of democracy, and the black American soldier has himself never experienced democracy.

While the war devours the young abroad, at home urban outbreaks pit black youth against young soldiers and guardsmen, as racial and economic injustice exhaust human endurance. Prosperity gluts the middle and upper classes, while poverty imprisons more than thirty million Americans and starvation literally stalks rural areas of the South.

Crime rises in every segment of society. As diseases are conquered and health improved, mass drug consumption and alcoholism assume epidemic proportions.

The alienation of young people from society rises to unprecedented levels, and masses of voluntary exiles emerge as modern gypsies, aimless and empty.

This generation is engaged in a cold war, not only with the earlier generation, but with the values of its society. It is not the familiar and normal hostility of the young groping for independence. It has a new quality of bitter antagonism and confused anger, which suggests basic issues are being contested.

These are unprecedented attitudes because this generation was born and matured in unprecedented conditions.

The generation of the past twenty-five years cannot be understood without remembering that it has lived during that period through the effects of four wars: World War II, the "cold war," the Korean War, and Vietnam. No other generation of young Americans was ever exposed to a remotely similar traumatic experience. Yet as spiritually and physically abrasive as this may be, it is not the worst aspect of contemporary experience. This is the first generation to grow up in the era of the nuclear bomb, knowing that it may be the last generation of mankind.

This is the generation not only of war, but of war in its ultimate revelation. This is the generation that truly has no place to hide and no place to find security.

These are evils enough to send reason reeling. And of course they are not the only ones. All of them form part of the matrix in which this generation's character and experience were formed. The tempest of evils provides the answer for those adults who ask why this young generation is so unfathomable, so alienated, and frequently so freakish. For the young people of today, peace and social tranquillity are as unreal and remote as knight-errantry.

Under the impact of social forces unique to their times, young people have splintered into three principal groups, though of course there is some overlap among the three.

The largest group of young people is struggling to adapt itself to the prevailing values of our society. Without much enthusiasm, they accept the system of government, the economic relationships of the property system, and the social stratifications both engender. But even so, they are a profoundly troubled group, and are harsh critics of the *status quo*.

In this largest group, social attitudes are not congealed or determined; they are fluid and searching. Though all recent studies point to the fact that the war in Vietnam is a focus of concern, most of them are not ready to resist the draft or to take clear-cut stands on issues of violence and nonviolence. But their consciences have been touched by the feeling that is growing, all over the world, of the horror and insanity of war, of the imperative need to respect life, of the urgency of moving past war as a way to solve international problems. So while they will not glorify war, and while they feel ambiguous about America's military posture, this majority group reflects the confusion of the larger society, which is itself caught up in a kind of transitional state of conscience as it moves slowly toward the realization that war cannot be justified in the human future.

There is a second group of young people, the radicals. They range from moderate to extreme in the degree to which they want to alter the social system. All of them agree that only by *structural* change can current evils be eliminated, because the roots are in the system rather than in men or in faulty operation. These are a new breed of radicals. Very few adhere to any established ideology; some borrow from old doctrines of revolution; but practically all of them suspend judgment on what the form of a new society must be. They are in serious revolt against old values and have not yet concretely formulated the new ones. They are not repeating previous revolutionary doctrines; most of them have not even read the revolutionary classics. Ironically, their rebelliousness comes from having been frustrated in seeking change within the framework of the existing society. They tried to build racial equality and met tenacious and vicious opposition. They worked to end the Vietnam war and experienced futility. So they seek a fresh start with new rules in a new order. It is fair to say, though, that at present they know what they don't want rather than what they do want. Their radicalism is growing because the power structure of today is unrelenting in defending not only its social system but the evils it contains; so, naturally, it is intensifying the opposition.

What is the attitude of this second radical group to the problem of violence? In a word, mixed; there are young radicals today who are pacifists, and there are others who are armchair revolutionaries who insist on the political and psychological need for violence. These young theorists of violence elaborately scorn the process of dialogue in favour of the "tactics of confrontation"; they glorify the guerrilla movement and especially its new martyr, Che Guevara; and they equate revolutionary consciousness with the readiness to shed blood. But across the spectrum of attitudes toward violence that can be found among the radicals is there a unifying thread? I think there is. Whether they read Gandhi or Frantz Fanon, all the radicals understand the need for action—direct self-transforming and structure-transforming action. This may be their most creative, collective insight.

The young people in the third group are currently called "hippies". They may be traced in a fairly direct line from yesterday's beatniks. The hippies are not only colourful, but complex; and in many respects their extreme conduct illuminates the negative effect of society's evils on sensitive young people. While there are variations, those who identify with this group have a common philosophy. They are struggling to disengage from society as their expression of their rejection of it. They disavow responsibility to organized society. Unlike the radicals, they are seeking not change but flight. When occasionally they merge with a peace demonstration, it is not to better the political world, but to give expression to their own world. The hard-core hippie is a remarkable contradiction. He uses drugs to turn inward, away from reality, to find peace and security. Yet he advocates love as the highest human value—love, which can exist only in communication between people, and not in the total isolation of the individual.

The importance of the hippies is not in their

unconventional behaviour, but in the fact that some hundreds of thousands of young people, in turning to a flight from reality, are expressing a profoundly discrediting judgment on the society they emerge from.

It seems to me that the hippies will not last long as a mass group. They cannot survive because there is no solution in escape. Some of them may persist by solidifying into a secular religious sect; their movement already has many such characteristics. We might see some of them establish utopian colonies, like the seventeenth- and eighteenth-century communities established by sects that profoundly opposed the existing order and its values. Those communities did not survive. But they were important to their contemporaries because their dream of social justice and human value continues as a dream of mankind.

In this context, one dream of the hippie group is very significant, and that is its dream of peace. Most of the hippies are pacifists, and a few have thought their way through to a persuasive and psychologically sophisticated "peace strategy". And society at large may be more ready now to learn from that dream than it was a century or two ago, to listen to the argument for peace, not as a dream, but as a practical possibility: something to choose and use.

From this quick tour of the three main groupings of our young people, it should be evident that this generation is in substantial ferment. Even the large group that is not disaffected from society is putting forward basic questions, and its restlessness helps us understand the radicals with their angry protest and the hippies with their systematic withdrawal.

When the less sensitive supporters of the *status quo* try to argue against some of these condemnations and challenges, they usually cite the technological marvels our society has achieved. However, that only reveals their poverty of spirit. Mammoth productive facilities with computer minds, cities that engulf the landscape and pierce the clouds, planes that almost outrace time—these are awesome, but they cannot be spiritually inspiring. Nothing in our glittering technology can raise man to new heights, because material growth has been made an end in itself, and, in the absence of moral purpose, man himself becomes smaller as the works of man become bigger.

Another distortion in the technological revolution is that, instead of strengthening democracy at home, it has helped to eviscerate it. Gargantuan industry and government, woven into an intricate computerized mechanism, leave the person outside. The sense of participation is lost, the feeling that ordinary individuals influence important decisions vanishes, and man becomes separated and diminished.

When an individual is no longer a true participant, when he no longer feels a sense of responsibility to his society, the content of democracy is emptied. When culture is degraded and vulgarity enthroned, when the social system does not build security but induces peril, inexorably the individual is impelled to pull away from a soulless society. This process produces alienation—perhaps the most pervasive and insidious development in contemporary society.

Alienation is not confined to our young people, but it is rampant among them. Yet alienation should be foreign to the young. Growth requires connection and trust. Alienation is a form of living death. It is the acid of despair that dissolves society.

Up to now, I have been looking at the tragic factors in the quarter-century of history that today's youth has lived through. But is there another side? Are there forces in that quarter-century that could reverse the process of alienation? We must now go back over those twenty-five years to search for positive ingredients which have been there, but in relative obscurity.

Against the exaltation of technology, there has always been a force struggling to respect higher values. None of the current evils rose without resistance, nor have they persisted without opposition.

During the early 1950s the hangman operating with the cold war troops was McCarthyism. For years it decimated social organizations, throttled free expression, and intimidated into bleak silence not only liberals and radicals but men in high and protected places. A very small band of courageous people fought back, braving ostracism, slander, and loss of livelihood. Gradually and painfully, however, the democratic instinct of Americans was awakened, and the ideological brute force was routed.

However, McCarthyism left a legacy of social paralysis. Fear persisted through succeeding years, and social reform remained inhibited and defensive. A blanket of conformity and intimidation conditioned young and old to exalt mediocrity and convention. Criticism of the social order was still imbued with implications of treason. The war in Korea was unpopular, but it was never subject to the searching criticisms and mass demonstrations that currently characterize opposition to the war in Vietnam.

The blanket of fear was lifted by Negro youth. When they took their struggle to the streets, a new spirit of resistance was born. Inspired by the boldness and ingenuity of Negroes, white youth stirred into action and formed an alliance that aroused the conscience of the nation.

It is difficult to exaggerate the creative contribution of young Negroes. They took nonviolent resistance, first employed in Montgomery, Alabama, in mass dimensions, and developed original forms of application—sit-ins, freedom rides, and wade-ins. To accomplish these, they first transformed themselves. Young Negroes had traditionally imitated whites in dress, conduct, and thought in a rigid, middle-class pattern. Gunnar Myrdal described them as exaggerated Americans. Now they ceased imitating and began initiating. Leadership passed into the hands of Negroes, and their white allies began learning from them. This was a revolutionary and wholesome development for both. It is ironic that today so many educators and sociologists are seeking methods to instil middle-class values in Negro youth as the ideal in social development. It was precisely when young Negroes threw off their middle-class values that they made an historic social contribution. They abandoned those values when they put careers and wealth in a secondary role. When they cheerfully became jailbirds and troublemakers, when they took off their Brooks Brothers attire and put on overalls to work in the isolated rural South, they challenged and inspired white youth to emulate them. Many left school, not to abandon learning, but to seek it in more direct ways. They were constructive school drop-outs, a variety that strengthened the society and themselves. These Negro and white youth preceded the conception of the Peace Corps, and it is safe to say that their work was the inspiration for its organization on an international scale.

The collective effort that was born out of the civil rights alliance was awesomely fruitful for this country in the first years of the 1960s. The repressive forces that had not been seriously challenged for almost a decade now faced an aroused adversary. A torrent of humanist thought and action swept across the land, scoring first small and then larger victories. The awakening grew in breadth, and the contested issues encompassed other social questions. A phalanx of reliable young activists took protest from hiding and revived a sense of responsible rebellion. A peace movement was born.

The Negro freedom movement would have been historic and worthy even if it had only served the cause of civil rights. But its laurels are greater because it stimulated a broader social movement that elevated the moral level of the nation. In the struggle against the preponderant evils of the society, decent values were preserved. Moreover, a significant body of young people learned that in opposing the tyrannical forces that were crushing them they added stature and meaning to their lives. The alliance of Negro and white youth that fought bruising engagements with the *status quo* inspired each other with a sense of moral mission, and both gave the nation an example of self-sacrifice and dedication.

These years—the late sixties—are a most crucial time for the movement I have been describing. There is a sense in which it can be said that the civil rights and peace movements are over—at least in their first form, the protest form, which gave them their first victories. There is a sense in which the alliance of responsible young people which the movement represented has fallen apart under the impact of failures, discouragement, and consequent extremism and polarization. The movement for social change has entered a time of temptation to despair because it is clear now how deep and systemic are the evils it confronts. There is a strong temptation to despair of programmes and action, and to dissipate energy in hysterical talk. There is a temptation to break up into mutually suspicious extremist groups, in which blacks reject the participation of whites and whites reject the realities of their own history.

But meanwhile, as the young people face this crisis, leaders in the movement are working out programmes to bring the social movements through from their early, and now inadequate, protest phase to a new stage of massive, active, nonviolent resistance to the evils of the modern system. As this work and this planning proceed, we begin to glimpse tremendous vistas of what it might mean for the world if the new programmes of resistance succeed in forging an even wider alliance of today's awakened youth.

Nonviolent active resistance to social evils, including massive civil disobedience when there is need for it, can unite in a new action-synthesis the best insights of all three groups I have pointed out among our young people. From the hippies, it can accept the vision of peaceful means to a goal of peace, and also their sense of beauty, gentleness, and of the unique gifts of each man's spirit. From the radicals, it can adopt the burning sense of urgency, the recognition of the need for direct and collective action, and the need for strategy and organization. And because the emerging programme is neither one of anarchy nor one of despair, it can welcome the work and insights of those young people who have not rejected our present society in its totality. They can challenge the more extreme groups to integrate the new vision into history as it actually is, into society as it actually works. They can help the movement not to break the bruised reed or to quench the smoking wick of values that are already recognized in the society that we want to change. And they can help keep open the possibility of honourable compromise.

If the early civil rights movement bore some international fruit in the formation of a Peace Corps, this new alliance could do far more. Already our best young workers in the United States are talking about the need to organize in international dimensions. They are beginning to form conscious connections with their opposite numbers in other countries. The conscience of an awakened activist cannot be satisfied with a focus on local problems, if only because he sees that local problems are all interconnected with world problems. The young men who are beginning to see that they must refuse to leave their country in order to fight and kill others might decide to leave their country, at least for a while, in order to share their life with others. There is as yet not even an outline in existence of what structure this growing world-consciousness might find for itself. But a dozen years ago there was not even an outline for the Negro civil rights movement in its first phase. The spirit is awake now; structures will follow, if we keep our eyes open to the spirit. Perhaps the structural forms will emerge from other countries, propelled by another experience of the shaping of history.

But we do not have much time. The revolutionary spirit is already world-wide. If the anger of the peoples of the world at the injustice of things is to be channelled into a revolution of love and creativity, we must begin now to work, urgently, with all the peoples, to shape a new world.

IV

NONVIOLENCE
AND
SOCIAL
CHANGE

THERE is nothing wrong with a traffic law which says you have to stop for a red light. But when a fire is raging, the fire truck goes right through that red light, and normal traffic had better get out of its way. Or, when a man is bleeding to death, the ambulance goes through those red lights at top speed.

There is a fire raging now for the Negroes and the poor of this society. They are living in tragic conditions because of the terrible economic injustices that keep them locked in as an "underclass," as the sociologists are now calling it. Disinherited people all over the world are bleeding to death from deep social and economic wounds. They need brigades of ambulance drivers who will have to ignore the red lights of the present system until the emergency is solved.

Massive civil disobedience is a strategy for social change which is at least as forceful as an ambulance with its siren on full. In the past ten years, nonviolent civil disobedience has made a great deal of history, especially in the Southern United States. When we and the Southern Christian Leadership Conference went to Birmingham, Alabama, in 1963, we had decided to take action on the matter of integrated public accommodations. We went knowing that the Civil Rights Commission had written powerful documents calling for change, calling for the very rights we were demanding. But nobody did anything about the Commission's report. Nothing was done until we acted on these very issues, and demonstrated before the court of world opinion the urgent need for change. It was the same story with voting rights. The Civil Rights Commission, three years before we went to Selma, had recommended the changes we started marching for, but nothing was done until, in 1965, we created a crisis the nation couldn't ignore. Without violence, we totally disrupted the system, the life style of Birmingham, and then of Selma, with their unjust and unconstitutional laws. Our Birmingham struggle came to its dramatic climax when some 3,500 demonstrators virtually filled every jail in that city and surrounding communities, and some 4,000 more continued to march and demonstrate nonviolently. The city knew then in terms that were crystal-clear that Birmingham could no longer continue to function until the demands of the Negro community were met. The same kind of dramatic crisis was created in Selma two years later. The result on the national scene was the Civil Rights Bill and the

Voting Rights Act, as President and Congress responded to the drama and the creative tension generated by the carefully planned demonstration.

Of course, by now it is obvious that new laws are not enough. The emergency we now face is economic, and it is a desperate and worsening situation. For the 35 million poor people in America—not even to mention, just yet, the poor in the other nations—there is a kind of strangulation in the air. In our society it is murder, psychologically, to deprive a man of a job or an income. You are in substance saying to that man that he has no right to exist. You are in a real way depriving him of life, liberty, and the pursuit of happiness, denying in his case the very creed of his society. Now, millions of people are being strangled that way. The problem is international in scope. And it is getting worse, as the gap between the poor and the "affluent society" increases.

The question that now divides the people who want radically to change that situation is: can a programme of nonviolence—even if it envisions massive civil disobedience—realistically expect to meet such an enormous, entrenched evil?

First of all, will nonviolence work, psychologically, after the summer of 1967? Many people feel that nonviolence as a strategy for social change was cremated in the flames of the urban riots of the last two years. They tell us that Negroes have only now begun to find their true manhood in violence; that the riots prove not only that Negroes hate whites, but that, compulsively, they must destroy them.

This blood-lust interpretation ignores one of the most striking features of the city riots. Violent they certainly were. But the violence, to a startling degree, was focussed against property rather than against people. There were very few cases of injury to persons, and the vast majority of the rioters were not involved at all in attacking people. The much publicized "death toll" that marked the riots, and the many injuries, were overwhelmingly inflicted on the rioters by the military. It is clear that the riots were exacerbated by police action that was designed to injure or even to kill people. As for the snipers, no account of the riots claims that more than one or two dozen people were involved in sniping. From the facts, an unmistakable pattern emerges: a handful of Negroes used gunfire substantially to intimidate, not to kill; and all of the other participants had a different target—property.

I am aware that there are many who wince at a distinction between property and persons—who hold both sacrosanct. My views are not so rigid. A life is sacred. Property is intended to serve life, and no matter how much we surround it with rights and respect, it has no personal being. It is part of the earth man walks on; it is not man.

The focus on property in the 1967 riots is not accidental. It has a message; it is saying something.

If hostility to whites were ever going to dominate a Negro's attitude and reach murderous proportions, surely it would be during a riot. But this rare opportunity for bloodletting was sublimated into arson, or turned into a kind of stormy carnival of free-merchandise distribution. Why did the rioters avoid personal attacks? The explanation cannot be fear of retribution, because the physical risks incurred in the attacks on property were no less than for personal assaults. The military forces were treating acts of petty larceny as equal to murder. Far more rioters took chances with their own lives, in their attacks on property, than threatened the life of anyone else. Why were they so violent with property then? Because property represents the white power structure, which they were attacking and trying to destroy. A curious proof of the symbolic aspect of the looting for some who took part in it is the fact that, after the riots, police received hundreds of calls from Negroes trying to return merchandise they had taken. Those people wanted the experience of taking, of redressing the power imbalance that property represents. Possession, afterward, was secondary.

A deeper level of hostility came out in arson, which was far more dangerous than the looting. But it, too, was a demonstration and a warning. It was directed against symbols of exploitation, and it was designed to express the depth of anger in the community.

What does this restraint in the summer riots mean for our future strategy?

If one can find a core of nonviolence towards persons, even during the riots when emotions were exploding, it means that nonviolence should not be written off for the future as a force in Negro life. Many people believe that the urban Negro is too angry and too sophisticated to be nonviolent. Those same people dismiss the nonviolent marches in the South and try to describe them as processions of pious, elderly ladies. The fact is that in all the marches we have organized some men of very violent tendencies have been involved. It was routine for us to collect hundreds of knives from our own ranks before the demonstrations, in case of momentary weakness. And in Chicago last year we saw some of the most violent individuals accepting nonviolent discipline. Day after day during those Chicago marches I walked in our lines and I never saw anyone retaliate with violence. There were lots of provocations, not only the screaming white hoodlums lining the sidewalks, but also groups of Negro militants talking about guerrilla warfare. We had some gang leaders and members marching with us. I remember walking with the Blackstone Rangers while bottles were flying from the sidelines, and I saw their noses being broken and blood flowing from their wounds; and I saw them continue and not retaliate, not one of them, with violence. I am convinced that even very violent temperaments can be channelled through nonviolent discipline, if the movement is moving, if they can act constructively and express through an effective channel their very legitimate anger.

But even if nonviolence can be valid, psychologically, for the protesters who want change, is it going to be effective, strategically, against a government and a *status quo* that have so far resisted this summer's demands on the grounds that "we must not reward the rioters"? Far from rewarding the rioters, far from even giving a hearing to their just and urgent demands, the administration has ignored its responsibility for the causes of the riots, and instead has used the negative aspects of them to justify continued inaction on the underlying issues. The administration's only concrete response was to initiate a study and call for a day of prayer. As a minister, I take prayer too seriously to use it as an excuse for avoiding work and responsibility. When a government commands more wealth and power than has ever been known in the history of the world, and offers no more than this, it is worse than blind, it is provocative. It is paradoxical but fair to say that Negro terrorism is incited less on ghetto street corners than in the halls of Congress.

I intended to show that nonviolence will be effective, but not until it has achieved the massive dimensions, the disciplined planning, and the intense commitment of a sustained, direct-action movement of civil disobedience on the national scale.

The dispossessed of this nation—the poor, both white and Negro—live in a cruelly unjust society. They must organize a revolution against that injustice, not against the lives of the persons who are their fellow citizens, but against the structures through which the society is refusing to take means which have been called for, and which are at hand, to lift the load of poverty.

The only real revolutionary, people say, is a man who has nothing to lose. There are millions of poor people in this country who have very little, or even nothing, to lose. If they can be helped to take action together, they will do so with a freedom and a power that will be a new and unsettling force in our complacent national life. Beginning in the New Year, we will be recruiting three thousand of the poorest citizens from ten different urban and rural areas to initiate and lead a sustained, massive, direct-action movement in Washington. Those who choose to join this initial three thousand, this nonviolent army, this "freedom church" of the poor, will work with us for three months to develop nonviolent action skills. Then we will move on Washington, determined to stay there until the legislative and executive branches of the government take serious and adequate action on jobs and income. A delegation of poor people can walk into a high official's office with a carefully, collectively prepared list of demands. (If you're poor, if you're unemployed anyway, you can choose to stay in Washington as long as the struggle needs you.) And if that official says, "But Congress would have to approve this," or, "But the President would have to be consulted on that," you can say, "All right, we'll wait." And you can settle down in his office for as long a stay as necessary. If you are, let's say, from rural Mississippi, and have never had medical attention, and your children are undernourished and unhealthy, you can take those little children into the Washington hospitals and stay with them there until the medical workers cope with their needs, and in showing it your children you will have shown this country a sight that will make it stop in its busy tracks and think hard about what it has done. The many people who will come and join this three thousand, from all groups in the country's life, will play a supportive role, deciding to be poor for a time along with the dispossessed who are asking for their right to jobs or income—jobs, income, the demolition of slums, and the rebuilding by the people who live there of new communities in their place; in fact, a new economic deal for the poor.

Why camp in Washington to demand these things? Because only the federal Congress and administration can decide to use the billions of dollars we need for a real war on poverty. We need, not a new law, but a massive, new national programme. This Congress has done nothing to help such measures, and plenty to hinder them. Why should Congress care about our dying cities? It is still dominated by senior representatives of the rural South, who still unite in an obstructive coalition with unprogressive Northerners to prevent public funds from going where they are socially needed. We broke that coalition in 1963 and 1964, when the Civil Rights and Voting Rights laws were passed. We need to break it again by the size and force of our movement, and the best place to do that is before the eyes and inside the buildings of these same Congressmen.

The people of this country, if not the Congress-men, are ready for a serious economic attack on slums and unemployment, as two recent polls by Lou Harris have revealed. So we have to make Congress ready to act on the plight of the poor. We will prod and sensitize the legislators, the administrators, and all the wielders of power until they have faced this utterly imperative need.

I have said that the problem, the crisis we face, is international in scope. In fact, it is inseparable from an international emergency which involves the poor, the dispossessed, and the exploited of the whole world.

Can a nonviolent, direct-action movement find application on the international level, to con-front economic and political problems? I believe it can. It is clear to me that the next stage of the movement is to become international. National movements within the developed countries— forces that focus on London, or Paris, or Washing-ton, or Ottawa—must help to make it politically feasible for their governments to undertake the kind of massive aid that the developing countries need if they are to break the chains of poverty. We in the West must bear in mind that the poor countries are poor primarily because we have exploited them through political or economic colonialism. Americans in particular must help their nation repent of her modern economic imperialism.

But movements in our countries alone will not be enough. In Latin America, for example, national reform movements have almost despaired of nonviolent methods; many young men, even many priests, have joined guerrilla movements in the hills. So many of Latin America's problems have roots in the United States of America that we need to form a solid, united movement, nonviolently conceived and carried through, so that pressure can be brought to bear on the capital and government power structures concerned, from both sides of the problem at once. I think that may be the only hope for a nonviolent solution in Latin America today; and one of the most powerful expressions of nonviolence may come out of that international coalition of socially aware forces, operating outside governmental frameworks.

Even entrenched problems like the South African Government and its racial policies could be tackled on this level. If just two countries, Britain and the United States, could be persuaded to end all economic interaction with the South African regime, they could bring that government to its knees in a relatively short time. Theoretically, the British and American governments could make that kind of decision; almost every corporation in both countries has economic ties with its government which it could not afford to do without. In practice, such a decision would represent such a major reordering of priorities that we should not expect that any movement could bring it about in one year or two. Indeed, although it is obvious that nonviolent movements for social change must internationalize, because of the interlocking nature of the problems they all face, and because otherwise those problems will breed war, we have hardly begun to build the skills and the strategy, or even the commitment, to planetize our movement for social justice.

In a world facing the revolt of ragged and hungry masses of God's children; in a world torn between the tensions of East and West, white and coloured, individualists and collectivists; in a world whose cultural and spiritual power lags so far behind her technological capabilities that we live each day on the verge of nuclear co-annihilation; in this world, nonviolence is no longer an option for intellectual analysis, it is an imperative for action.

V

A
CHRISTMAS
SERMON
ON
PEACE

PEACE on earth . . .

This Christmas season finds us a rather bewildered human race. We have neither peace within nor peace without. Everywhere paralysing fears harrow people by day and haunt them by night. Our world is sick with war; everywhere we turn we see its ominous possibilities. And yet, my friends, the Christmas hope for peace and goodwill toward all men can no longer be dismissed as a kind of pious dream of some utopian. If we don't have goodwill toward men in this world, we will destroy ourselves by the misuse of our own instruments and our own power. Wisdom born of experience should tell us that war is obsolete. There may have been a time when war served as a negative good by preventing the spread and growth of an evil force, but the very destructive power of modern weapons of war—

The text of this chapter was delivered by Dr. King as a Christmas sermon in Ebenezer Baptist Church at Atlanta, Georgia, and was broadcast by CBC as the final Massey Lecture, on Christmas Eve, 1967.

fare eliminates even the possibility that war may any longer serve as a negative good. And so, if we assume that life is worth living, if we assume that mankind has a right to survive, then we must find an alternative to war—and so let us this morning explore the conditions for peace. Let us this morning think anew on the meaning of that Christmas hope: "Peace on Earth, Good Will toward Men." And as we explore these conditions, I would like to suggest that modern man really go all out to study the meaning of nonviolence, its philosophy and its strategy.

We have experimented with the meaning of nonviolence in our struggle for racial justice in the United States, but now the time has come for man to experiment with nonviolence in all areas of human conflict, and that means nonviolence on an international scale.

Now let me suggest first that if we are to have peace on earth, our loyalties must become ecumenical rather than sectional. Our loyalties must transcend our race, our tribe, our class, and our nation; and this means we must develop a world perspective. No individual can live alone; no nation can live alone, and as long as we try, the more we are going to have war in this world. Now the judgment of God is upon us, and we must either learn to live together as brothers or we are all going to perish together as fools.

Yes, as nations and individuals, we are inter-dependent. I have spoken to you before of our visit to India some years ago. It was a marvellous experience; but I say to you this morning that there were those depressing moments. How can one avoid being depressed when one sees with one's own eyes evidences of millions of people going to bed hungry at night? How can one avoid being depressed when one sees with one's own eyes thousands of people sleeping on the sidewalks at night? More than a million people sleep on the sidewalks of Bombay every night; more than half a million sleep on the sidewalks of Calcutta every night. They have no houses to go into. They have no beds to sleep in. As I beheld these conditions, something within me cried out: "Can we in America stand idly by and not be concerned?" And an answer came: "Oh, no!" And I started thinking about the fact that right here in our country we spend millions of dollars every day to store surplus food; and I said to myself: "I know where we can store that food free of charge —in the wrinkled stomachs of the millions of God's children in Asia, Africa, Latin America, and even in our own nation, who go to bed hungry at night."

It really boils down to this: that all life is inter-related. We are all caught in an inescapable network of mutuality, tied into a single garment of destiny. Whatever affects one directly, affects all indirectly. We are made to live together because of the inter-related structure of reality. Did you ever stop to think that you can't leave for your job in the morning without being dependent on most of the world? You get up in the morning and go to the bathroom and reach over for the sponge, and that's handed to you by a Pacific islander. You reach for a bar of soap, and that's given to you at the hands of a Frenchman. And then you go into the kitchen to drink your coffee for the morning, and that's poured into your cup by a South American. And maybe you want tea: that's poured into your cup by a Chinese. Or maybe you're desirous of having cocoa for breakfast, and that's poured into your cup by a West African. And then you reach over for your toast, and that's given to you at the hands of an English-speaking farmer, not to mention the baker. And before you finish eating breakfast in the morning, you've depended on more than half of the world. This is the way our universe is structured, this is its inter-related quality. We aren't going to have peace on earth until we recognize this basic fact of the inter-related structure of all reality.

Now let me say, secondly, that if we are to have peace in the world, men and nations must embrace the nonviolent affirmation that ends and means must cohere. One of the great philosophi-

cal debates of history has been over the whole
question of means and ends. And there have
always been those who argued that the end justifies the means, that the means really aren't important. The important thing is to get to the
end, you see.

So, if you're seeking to develop a just society,
they say, the important thing is to get there, and
the means are really unimportant; any means will
do so long as they get you there—they may be
violent, they may be untruthful means; they may
even be unjust means to a just end. There have
been those who have argued this throughout history. But we will never have peace in the world
until men everywhere recognize that ends are not
cut off from means, because the means represent
the ideal in the making, and the end in process,
and ultimately you can't reach good ends through
evil means, because the means represent the seed
and the end represents the tree.

It's one of the strangest things that all the great
military geniuses of the world have talked about
peace. The conquerors of old who came killing in
pursuit of peace, Alexander, Julius Caesar, Char-
lemagne, and Napoleon, were akin in seeking a
peaceful world order. If you will read *Mein
Kampf* closely enough, you will discover that Hit-
ler contended that everything he did in Germany
was for peace. And the leaders of the world today

talk eloquently about peace. Every time we drop our bombs in North Vietnam, President Johnson talks eloquently about peace. What is the problem? They are talking about peace as a distant goal, as an end we seek, but one day we must come to see that peace is not merely a distant goal we seek, but that it is a means by which we arrive at that goal. We must pursue peaceful ends through peaceful means. All of this is saying that, in the final analysis, means and ends must cohere because the end is pre-existent in the means, and ultimately destructive means cannot bring about constructive ends.

Now let me say that the next thing we must be concerned about if we are to have peace on earth and goodwill toward men is the nonviolent affirmation of the sacredness of all human life. Every man is somebody because he is a child of God. And so when we say "Thou shalt not kill," we're really saying that human life is too sacred to be killed on the battlefields of the world. Man is more than a tiny vagary of whirling electrons or a wisp of smoke from a limitless smouldering. Man is a child of God, made in His image, and therefore must be respected as such. Until men see this everywhere, until nations see this everywhere, we will be fighting wars. One day somebody should remind us that, even though there may be political and ideological differences between us, the Vietnamese are our brothers, the Russians are our brothers, the Chinese are our brothers; and one day we've got to sit down together at the table of brotherhood. But in Christ there is neither Jew nor Gentile. In Christ there is neither male nor female. In Christ there is neither Communist nor capitalist. In Christ, somehow, there is neither bound nor free. We are all one in Christ Jesus. And when we truly believe in the sacredness of human personality, we won't exploit people, we won't trample over people with the iron feet of oppression, we won't kill anybody.

There are three words for "love" in the Greek New Testament; one is the word *"eros."* *Eros* is a sort of aesthetic, romantic love. Plato used to talk about it a great deal in his dialogues, the yearning of the soul for the realm of the divine. And there is and can always be something beautiful about *eros*, even in its expressions of romance. Some of the most beautiful love in all of the world has been expressed this way.

Then the Greek language talks about *"philos,"* which is another word for love, and *philos* is a kind of intimate love between personal friends. This is the kind of love you have for those people that you get along with well, and those whom you like on this level you love because you are loved.

Then the Greek language had another word for love, and that is the word *"agapē."* *Agapē* is more than romantic love, it is more than friendship. *Agapē* is understanding, creative, redemptive goodwill toward all men. *Agapē* is an overflowing love which seeks nothing in return. Theologians would say that it is the love of God operating in the human heart. When you rise to love on this level, you love all men not because you like them, not because their ways appeal to you, but you love them because God loves them. This is what Jesus meant when He said, "Love your enemies." And I'm happy that He didn't say, "Like your enemies," because there are some people that I find it pretty difficult to like. Liking is an affectionate emotion, and I can't like anybody who would bomb my home. I can't like anybody who would exploit me. I can't like anybody who would trample over me with injustices. I can't like them. I can't like anybody who threatens to kill me day in and day out. But Jesus reminds us that love is greater than liking. Love is understanding, creative, redemptive goodwill toward all men. And I think this is where we are as a people, in our struggle for racial justice. We can't ever give up. We must work passionately and unrelentingly for first-class citizenship. We must never let up in our determination to remove every vestige of segregation and discrimination from our nation, but we shall not in the process relinquish our privilege to love.

I've seen too much hate to want to hate, myself, and I've seen hate on the faces of too many sheriffs, too many white citizens' councillors, and too many Klansmen of the South to want to hate, myself; and every time I see it, I say to myself, hate is too great a burden to bear. Somehow we must be able to stand up before our most bitter opponents and say: "We shall match your capacity to inflict suffering by our capacity to endure suffering. We will meet your physical force with soul force. Do to us what you will and we will still love you. We cannot in all good conscience obey your unjust laws and abide by the unjust system, because non-cooperation with evil is as much a moral obligation as is cooperation with good, and so throw us in jail and we will still love you. Bomb our homes and threaten our children, and, as difficult as it is, we will still love you. Send your hooded perpetrators of violence into our communities at the midnight hour and drag us out on some wayside road and leave us half-dead as you beat us, and we will still love you. Send your propaganda agents around the country, and make it appear that we are not fit, culturally and otherwise, for integration, but we'll still love you. But be assured that we'll wear you down by our capacity to suffer, and one day we will win our freedom. We will not only win freedom for ourselves, we will so appeal to your heart and conscience that we will win you in the process, and our victory will be a double victory."

If there is to be peace on earth and goodwill toward men, we must finally believe in the ultimate morality of the universe, and believe that all reality hinges on moral foundations. Something must remind us of this as we once again stand in the Christmas season and think of the Easter season simultaneously, for the two somehow go together. Christ came to show us the way. Men love darkness rather than the light, and they crucified Him, and there on Good Friday on the Cross it was still dark, but then Easter came, and Easter is an eternal reminder of the fact that truth-crushed earth will rise again. Easter justifies Carlyle in saying, "No lie can live for ever." And so this is our faith, as we continue to hope for peace on earth and goodwill toward men: let us know that in the process we have cosmic companionship.

In 1963, on a sweltering August afternoon, we stood in Washington, D.C., and talked to the nation about many things. Toward the end of that afternoon, I tried to talk to the nation about a dream that I had had, and I must confess to you today that not long after talking about that dream I started seeing it turn into a nightmare. I remember the first time I saw that dream turn into a nightmare, just a few weeks after I had talked about it. It was when four beautiful, un-offending, innocent Negro girls were murdered in a church in Birmingham, Alabama. I watched that dream turn into a nightmare as I moved through the ghettos of the nation and saw my black brothers and sisters perishing on a lonely island of poverty in the midst of a vast ocean of material prosperity, and saw the nation doing nothing to grapple with the Negroes' problem of poverty. I saw that dream turn into a nightmare as I watched my black brothers and sisters in the midst of anger and understandable outrage, in the midst of their hurt, in the midst of their dis-appointment, turn to misguided riots to try to solve that problem. I saw that dream turn to a nightmare as I watched the war in Vietnam escalating, and as I saw so-called military advisers, 16,000 strong, turn into fighting soldiers until today over 500,000 American boys are fighting on Asian soil. Yes, I am personally the victim of de-ferred dreams, of blasted hopes, but in spite of that I close today by saying I still have a dream, because, you know, you can't give up in life. If you lose hope, somehow you lose that vitality that keeps life moving, you lose that courage to be, that quality that helps you to go on in spite of all. And so today I still have a dream.

I have a dream that one day men will rise up and come to see that they are made to live together as brothers. I still have a dream this morning that one day every Negro in this country, every coloured person in the world, will be judged on the basis of the content of his character rather than the colour of his skin, and every man will respect the dignity and worth of human personality. I still have a dream today that one day the idle industries of Appalachia will be revitalized, and the empty stomachs of Mississippi will be filled, and brotherhood will be more than a few words at the end of a prayer, but rather the first order of business on every legislative agenda. I still have a dream today that one day justice will roll down like water, and righteousness like a mighty stream. I still have a dream today that in all of our state houses and city halls men will be elected to go there who will do justly and love mercy and walk humbly with their God. I still have a dream today that one day war will come to an end, that men will beat their swords into ploughshares and their spears into pruning hooks, that nations will no longer rise up against nations, neither will they study war any more. I still have a dream today that one day the lamb and the lion will lie down together and every man will sit under his own vine and fig tree and none shall be afraid. I still have a dream today that one day every valley shall be exalted and every mountain and hill will be made low, the rough places will be made smooth and the crooked places straight, and the glory of the Lord shall be revealed, and all flesh shall see it together. I still have a dream that with this faith we will be able to adjourn the councils of despair and bring new light into the dark chambers of pessimism. With this faith we will be able to speed up the day when there will be peace on earth and goodwill toward men. It will be a glorious day, the morning stars will sing together, and the sons of God will shout for joy.

CORETTA SCOTT KING

My Life with Martin Luther King, Jr.

Martin Luther King is one of the twentieth century's immortals. His life and his death cast an influence not only on his own country but on the world. His wife's story of their life together is a unique document for that reason alone. It describes a relationship between two people who had vastly more reason than most to appreciate the meaning of 'human dignity' – a relationship that had always to be based on the knowledge that death might be imminent. Mrs King writes: 'My husband did not seek death, but once you commit yourself to an important cause, you cannot stop. You cannot say suddenly, "If I take this action, it will bring about my death." Instead you say, "If death is the price I have to pay, if death is a part of this commitment and this dedication, then my death may help to bring about those things I believe in." '

This is the story of a movement as well as of a family; of the special strains that work on a family when its head must dare hatred, humiliation, and, finally, death, for the ideas he represents. Yet the love that Martin Luther King and his wife brought to their marriage was able to transcend these difficulties. Their high points and their low points; the winning of the Nobel Peace Prize and the struggle to take their children to the local playground, are told by a brave and articulate woman whose strength played a vital role in her husband's life. This book will serve to take his message to hundreds of thousands of people whom an assassin's bullet prevented from seeing at first hand one of the truly great men of our time.

SBN 340 12907 7
Illustrated | 35s net